My Favourite Dogs

BOXER

Jinny Johnson

FRANKLIN WATTS
LONDON•SYDNEY

 An Appleseed Editions book

First published in 2013 by Franklin Watts
338 Euston Road, London NW1 3BH

© 2012 Appleseed Editions

Created by Appleseed Editions Ltd,
Well House, Friars Hill, Guestling,
East Sussex TN35 4ET

Designed and illustrated by Hel James
Edited by Mary-Jane Wilkins

ISBN 978 1 4451 2182 6

Dewey Classification: 636.7'3

A CIP catalogue for this book is available from the British Library.

Photo acknowledgements
t = top, b = bottom
page 1 guillermo77/Shutterstock; 3 Jeff Thrower/Shutterstock; 4 Karen Givens/
Shutterstock; 5 AnetaPics/Shutterstock; 6 Jupiterimages/Thinkstock; 7 Hemera/
Thinkstock; 8-9 Lebedinski Vladislav/Shutterstock; 11 Whytock/Shutterstock;
12 iStockphoto/Thinkstock; 13t iStockphoto/Thinkstock, b Linn Currie/Shutterstock;
14 Joy Brown/Shutterstock; 15 cynoclub/Shutterstock; 16 Hemera/Thinkstock;
17 Jana Behr/Shutterstock, b Hemera/Thinkstock; 18 Mars Evis/Shutterstock;
19 Anna Hoychuk/Shutterstock; 20 Hemera/Thinkstock; 21 iStockphoto/Thinkstock;
22-23 AnetaPics/Shutterstock; 23 Lenkadan/Shutterstock
Cover Nate A./Shutterstock

Printed in China

Franklin Watts is a division of Hachette Children's Books,
an Hachette UK company.
www.hachette.co.uk

Contents

I'm a boxer!

I'm handsome, loving
and fun to be with.
I'll be your loyal friend,
playmate and protector.

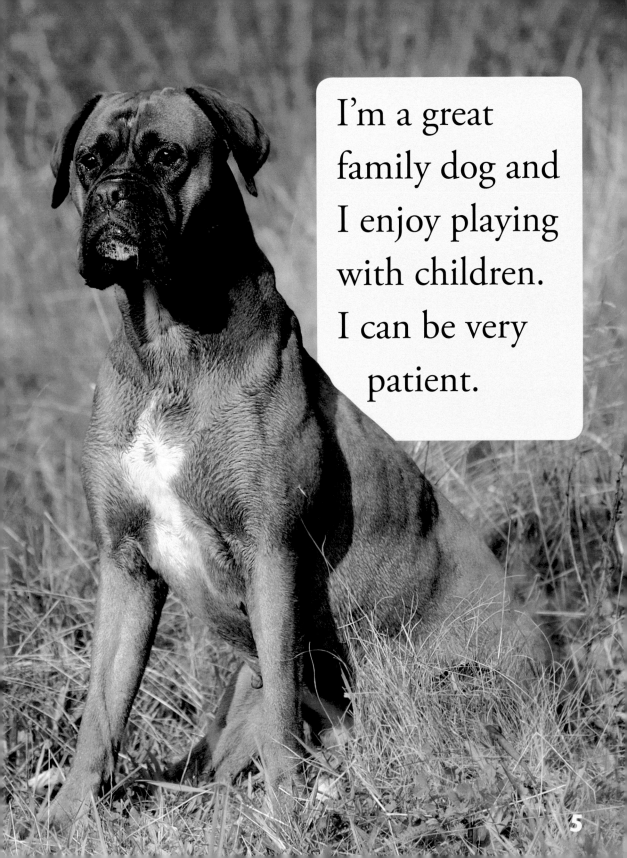

I'm a great family dog and I enjoy playing with children. I can be very patient.

5

What I need

I'm bouncy and full of energy, so I need plenty of exercise every day. I like to run and play games, and I love to clown around sometimes, too.

I'm happiest when I'm with people and I like being petted and cuddled. I get sad if I'm left alone too long.

The boxer

Smooth short coat

Tail often docked (trimmed) at birth

Tight skin

Colour: fawn or brindle (brownish with streaks of other colours) with white

Height: 54.5–63.5 cm

Weight: 25–32 kg

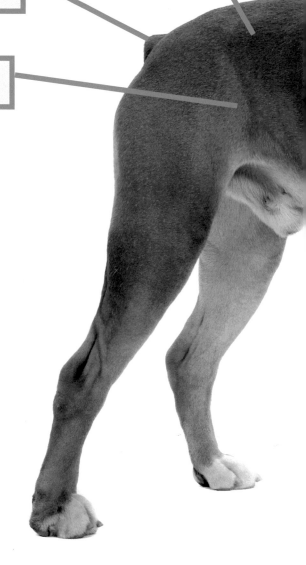

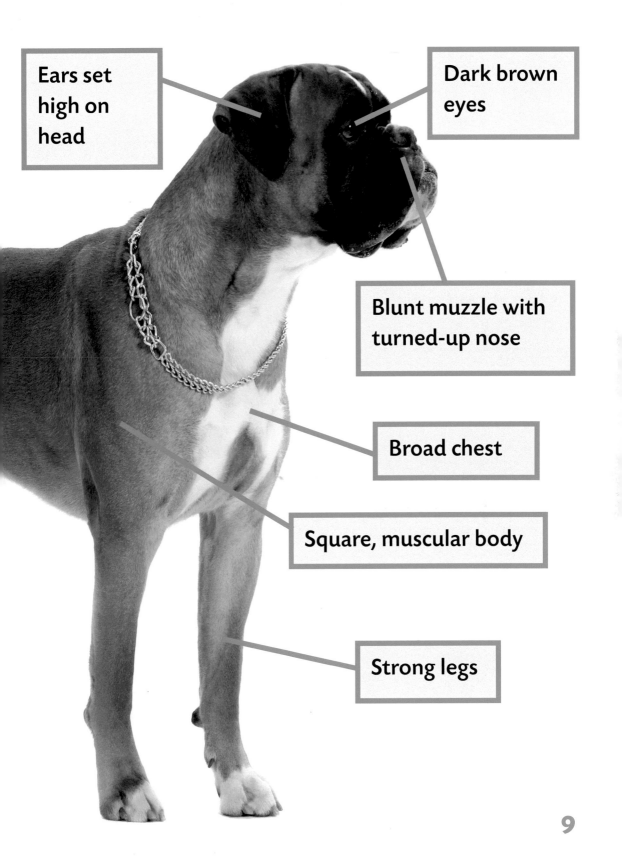

Ears set high on head

Dark brown eyes

Blunt muzzle with turned-up nose

Broad chest

Square, muscular body

Strong legs

9

All about boxers

Boxers are related to bulldogs. They were first bred in Germany in the 1800s for hunting animals such as deer.

Boxers are not used for hunting today, but they are brave, intelligent animals. They make good guard dogs and will defend the family.

Growing up

A boxer pup is an adorable bundle of energy that needs lots of attention.

A boxer pup will miss her mum when she first goes to her new home.

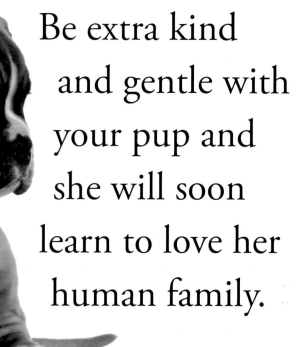

Be extra kind and gentle with your pup and she will soon learn to love her human family.

Be warned –
boxer pups love
to chew, so give
your puppy
plenty of toys.

Training your boxer

Boxers want to please their owners, but they can be stubborn so need careful training. Start training your boxer when she's young and always

show her who is boss. A well-trained boxer is a happy boxer.

Boxers are athletic dogs and they perform well at agility trials.

Working dogs

These dogs are intelligent, as well as strong, and often become working dogs. Boxers carried messages in wartime, and were one of the first breeds to be trained as police dogs.

Boxers also work as guide dogs and assistance dogs.

They love
to help
and protect
people.

Good company

Many boxer owners say their dogs are great company for all the family. Boxers show their feelings in their faces. Look at those eyes and that wrinkly forehead!

Boxers are very
good at sensing
moods. They love
to play when their owner
is happy, but they will cuddle
up and comfort you when they
feel you need it.

Your healthy boxer

A boxer has short hair and her coat only needs brushing once a week. She doesn't need a bath often either, unless she has rolled in something smelly.

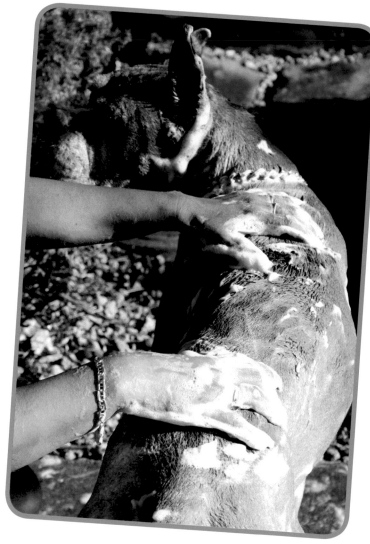

Boxers do not like very warm weather, so don't let your dog run too far and overheat on summer days.

Boxers can have hip problems, so have a puppy checked before buying. Get your boxer used to having her teeth cleaned when she is young, and brush them regularly.

Caring for your boxer

You and your family must think very carefully before buying a boxer. She may live as long as 11 years. Every day your dog must have food, water and exercise, as well as lots of love and care. She will also need to be taken to the vet for checks and vaccinations. When you go out or away, you must plan for your dog to be looked after.

Useful words

agility competitions
Events where dogs run round courses with obstacles and jumps.

breed
A particular type of dog.

vaccinations
Injections given by the vet to protect your dog against certain illnesses.

Index